INTO ADOLESCENCE:

Making and Keeping Friends

INTO ADOLESCENCE:

Making and Keeping Friends

A Curriculum for Grades 5-8

Emogene, Fox, EdD

Contemporary Health Series
Kathleen Middleton, MS, CHES, Series Editor

ETR Associates
Santa Cruz, California
1990

ETR Associates' Contemporary Health Series

Into Adolescence (for grades 5-8)

Choosing Abstinence
Enhancing Self-Esteem
Learning About AIDS
Learning About Reproduction and Birth
Living in a Family
A Time of Change (puberty)
Avoiding Drugs
Communicating Emotions
Becoming a Health-Wise Consumer
Making and Keeping Friends
Living Without Tobacco
Actions for Wellpower
Caring for Our Planet and Our Health
A Menu for Good Health
Fitness, Health and Hygiene
Stopping Violence

Entering Adulthood (for grades 9-12)

Connecting Health, Communication and Self-Esteem
Coping with Sexual Pressures
Living in Relationships
Preventing Sexually Related Disease
Understanding Reproduction, Birth and Contraception
Balancing Stress for Success
Understanding Depression and Suicide
Examining Drugs and Risks
Developing Responsibility and Self-Discipline
Planning Life Directions
Creating a Healthy Environment
Moving into Fitness
Looking at Body Image and Eating Disorders
Skills for Injury Prevention

Printed in the United States of America

10 9 8 7 6 5 4

Cover design: Julia Chiapella

Title No. 380

Illustrations:
p. 13 and 67 by Steven Baird
p. 93 by Ann Smiley

Library of Congress Cataloging-in-Publication Data

Fox, Emogene
   Into adolescence : making and keeping friends
      (Contemporary health series)
      Bibliography: p.
      1. Interpersonal relations in adolescence—Study and teaching
(Elementary).   2. Social skills—Study and teaching (Elementary)—
United States. I. Title. II. Series.

HM132.F94   1990   88-31408
ISBN 1-56071-016-0

This curriculum was made possible, in part, by a grant from the Walter S. Johnson Foundation. The opinions expressed in this curriculum are those of the author and do not necessarily reflect the opinions of the Walter S. Johnson Foundation.

DEDICATION

To my husband, Norris, my daughter, Dana, and my son, Jay, who are my best friends.

-EF

CONTENTS

EDITOR'S PREFACE
Contemporary Health Series

Health educators and practitioners know that prevention of health problems is far more desirable than treatment. The earlier the knowledge and skill to make healthful decisions are instilled, the greater the chance a healthful lifestyle will be adopted. School is the logical place in our society to provide children, adolescents and young adults the learning opportunities essential to developing the knowledge and skills to choose a healthful life course.

The **Contemporary Health Series** has been designed to provide educators with the curricular tools necessary to challenge students to take personal responsibility for their health. The long-range goals for the **Contemporary Health Series** are as follows:

Cognitive. Students will recognize the function of the existing body of knowledge pertaining to health and family life education.
Affective. Students will experience personal growth in the development of a positive self-concept and the ability to interact with others.
Practice. Students will gain skill in acting on personal decisions about health-related life choices.

Within the **Contemporary Health Series** there are two curricular divisions: *Into Adolescence* for middle school teachers and *Entering Adulthood* for high school teachers. The *Into Adolescence* modules focus on several different health and family life topics. Modules addressing puberty, AIDS, the family, self-esteem, reproduction and birth, sexual abstinence, friendship, emotions, nutrition, fitness, consumer choices, the environment, violence and drug, alcohol and tobacco education have been developed by skilled author/educators.

Entering Adulthood modules address reproduction and contraception, responsibility, stress, depression and suicide, life planning, communication and self-esteem, AIDS and other STDs, relationships, sexual abstinence, fitness, body image, the environment, injury prevention and drug, alcohol and tobacco education.

All the authors are, or have been, classroom teachers with particular expertise in each of the topic areas. They bring a unique combination of theory, content and practice resulting in curricula which weave educational learning theory into lessons appropriate for the developmental age of the student. The module format was chosen to facilitate flexibility as the modules are compatible with each other but may stand alone. Finally, ease of use by the classroom teacher has driven the design. The lessons are comprehensive, key components are clearly identified and masters for all student and teacher materials are provided.

The **Contemporary Health Series** is intended to help teachers address critical health issues in their classrooms. The beneficiaries are their students, our children, and the next generation.

Kathleen Middleton, MS, CHES
Series Editor

INTRODUCTION

A friendship is a warm relationship with another person you like and trust. Friends provide a basic source of happiness in general and a source of support in times of trouble. Friendships are important throughout life.

The ability to develop friendships during adolescence is especially important because they help ease the transition from childhood to adulthood. Page (1989) found that adolescents who have difficulty making and maintaining friendships are more susceptible to peer pressure and more likely to use drugs than adolescents who easily make friends and maintain friendships.

There are certain prerequisites to the development of meaningful, lasting friendships. Our friendships with others are founded on our own self-identity (understanding who we are), self-esteem (having positive feelings about ourselves) and sense of control (feeling in control of our lives).

The goal of this module is to provide students the opportunity for self-discovery, as well as to increase their understanding of others. Specifically, journal writing and other teaching strategies that complement student writing are used to encourage students to develop mental and social health education competencies (making and maintaining friendships) and critical thinking skills (using writing as a way to encourage higher-order thinking). Journal writing also enhances basic writing skills, because students practice writing without the threat of grading penalty.

As the author, I recognize that this module differs somewhat from other health education materials in its approach. But I hope it will provide students with a genuine learning experience that offers them the opportunity both to be creative and to have fun. I also hope each teacher who uses the module will find student journal writing an exciting teaching strategy and come to share my enthusiasm for it.

The module offers varied instructional strategies and lessons that are developmentally designed. Current theories and research on the dynamics of human development and the development of friendships have been used in the preparation of the curriculum.

Attempts have been made to make the curriculum culturally sensitive. The module is appropriate in any of the following classroom settings: health education, family life education, home economics and creative writing classes.

Overview

Activities in the first lesson help students recognize that individuals must know who they are, feel good about themselves and feel in control of their lives before they are able to develop meaningful friendships. In Lesson 2, students use journal writing and poetry writing to gain understanding about how they choose and maintain their friendships.

Lesson 3 deals with peer pressure and provides practice in saying no to risky behaviors without forfeiting friendships. Lesson 4 encourages students to look beyond a casual friendship to identify characteristics of a close friendship. Students also examine the behaviors needed to develop and maintain close personal friendships. In Lesson 5, students conduct interviews with parents or special adults and senior friends to learn about the lifelong significance of friendship. Lesson 6 serves as a culminating lesson. Students play a game about friendship and analyze what they learned about friendship in the previous lessons.

Objectives

Lesson 1   *Your Best Friend*

■ Students will be able to explain the importance of self-identity, self-esteem and a sense of control to developing friendships.

Lesson 2   *The Meaning of Friendship*

■ Students will be able to identify qualities they value in friends.

Lesson 3   *The Friends You Want*

■ Students will be able to describe ways that friends and peers influence personal choices and decisions.
■ Students will be able to identify some reasons to end a friendship.

Lesson 4	*Developing Close Friendships*	■ Students will be able to describe important skills to use in developing close friendships.
Lesson 5	*Friendship Through the Years*	■ Students will be able to describe the importance of friendship at different stages of life.
Lesson 6	*What I Learned About Friendship*	■ Students will be able to analyze the importance of friendship to them.

Time

The time indicated for each lesson is an approximate measure, based on a 45-50 minute class period. Actual time required to complete all the activities in the lesson will vary, depending on student interest and ability. Lessons that will probably require more than one class period to complete are indicated.

Instructional Strategies

Educators today are concerned that our students are not exercising what are often called higher-order thinking skills. This module addresses that concern through the use of a strategy called writing-to-learn. Here, this strategy is implemented mainly through journal writing.

Journal writing affords the opportunity for thinking and speculating on paper. This expressive writing requires that students combine learning and writing as they become actively (rather than passively) involved in the learning process.

Other instructional strategies, such as group discussion, brainstorming, cooperative learning activities, interviewing and publishing in the classroom are used to complement and expand journal writing. The specific strategies used in each lesson are clearly identified.

Journal Writing

This form of expressive writing is the kind of writing best adapted to exploration and discovery (Fulwiler, 1985). According to Nelms (1987), "Active learners process information. They do not merely receive it and give it back in the same form or in responses that require only recognition and recall. Active learners exercise what are often called the higher-order thinking skills. They apply, analyze, synthesize, evaluate, question, criticize and use information to solve problems. They use what they have learned to assist them in further learning."

Writing-to-learn, through the use of journal writing, is accomplished only if the writing is perceived as purposeful by the writer (Fulwiler, 1985). If writing is used largely for regurgitation, the writer sees it as a purposeless activity that requires only minimal involvement and effort.

Another counter-productive way of attempting to use writing-to-learn is to place too much initial stress on correctness (Mayer, Lester and Pradl, 1983). Writing cannot be an effective tool for learning if writers must worry about spelling and punctuation from the moment they put pen to paper. Journals should be places where students can try out their expressive voices freely, without fear of evaluation (Fulwiler, 1987).

Journal writing involves learners in building connections between what they are learning and what is already known (Mayer, Lester and Pradl, 1983). This form of expressive writing is effective because every time students write, they individualize instruction. The act of silent writing generates ideas, observations and emotions. Journal writing is used in this module to stimulate student discussion, start small-group activity, clarify hazy issues, reinforce learning experiences and evaluate student progress.

An alphabetical list of other instructional strategies and their description follows:

Brainstorming	Overhead Transparencies
Cooperative Learning	Publishing in the Classroom
Games	Roleplays
Group Discussion	Teacher Lecture
Interviewing	Worksheets

Brainstorming

Brainstorming is used to generate thoughts or discussion on an issue. If brainstorming is conducted as a class activity, the teacher should list everything that is said on the chalkboard or butcher paper. Brainstorming should continue until all ideas are exhausted or a predetermined time limit has been reached.

Cooperative Learning

Cooperative learning allows students to work together in small groups, sharing ownership, to create a written document. To insure the success of this teaching strategy, each group of students has a specific written task. The teacher serves as facilitator, moving about the groups, giving assistance when needed.

Games

A game is an amusing, sometimes competitive, educational activity that is played according to a specific set of rules.

Group Discussion

Group discussion offers the opportunity for peer interaction. This teaching strategy is used to analyze ideas and to process individual and group activities within the classroom. The size of the group is governed by the specific lesson being taught and the nature of the class. The process of determining group structure is vital to the success of the lessons. Groups may be created by student selection, random selection or selection based on ability. Once a group is formed, each member should have a responsibility in completing the group's larger task. While groups are working, the teacher should move from group to group, quietly observing, answering questions or facilitating any problem situations that occur.

Interviewing

In the quest for information on a topic, it is sometimes helpful to invite experts into the class or to interview others (family members or friends) outside of class. Advance preparation for an organized interview session increases the learning potential. A brainstorming session before the interview allows students to develop individual questions to ask during the interview.

Overhead Transparencies

Overhead transparencies offer an effective, highly visible way to present information and graphic examples. Most of these lessons provide teacher resources that can be used as transparencies.

Publishing in the Classroom

Publishing in the classroom is a mechanism for giving the writer an audience. It can be accomplished in the following ways:
- The teacher or students may read aloud (in small groups or to the entire class).
- With student permission, the teacher may select, duplicate and distribute examples of student writing. Journal selections should be published anonymously.
- Students choose their best writings (e.g., poetry) and bind them into individual or class books, which can then be shared.
- A bulletin board, wall or corner table may be used to create a classroom display for selected student writing.

Roleplays

Roleplays are highly motivating activities for students because they actively involve students in learning desired concepts or practicing certain behaviors. Students act out or act as if they are in a specific situation. Sometimes they are given a part to play, and other times they are given an idea and asked to improvise. Allow students time to decide the central action of the roleplay situation and how the roleplay will end.

Teacher Lecture

A traditional teacher lecture disseminates information directly from the teacher to students. In some lessons, this approach is the best way to provide information. Generally, this method is combined with other methods to assure high-level motivation and learning.

Worksheets

In some lessons, students are asked to complete worksheets. Worksheets are used in processing the activities of the lesson. Completed worksheets are then placed in the student's journal.

Groundrules

Groundrules should be established in the classroom before the lessons on friendship. This will help maintain a sensitive and positive atmosphere. It is usually helpful if students participate in the process of identifying the groundrules they want to follow during the lessons. One very important groundrule is that students have the right to pass on any question they feel is too personal for class discussion.

Evaluative Methods

Each lesson provides the teacher with one or more methods for evaluating student performance on stated objectives. The methods are listed following the Procedure section of each lesson. Evaluative methods include analysis and comment on worksheets and other written materials, as well as observation of individual responses.

It is impossible to objectively, quantitatively or qualitatively measure the development of personal friendship skills, and it is inappropriate to grade student work that is reflective of individual feelings, beliefs or behaviors. Therefore, the evaluative methods serve as tools to assess students' participation and cognitive learning from each lesson.

LESSON 1

YOUR BEST FRIEND

Objectives

Students will be able to explain the importance of self-identity, self-esteem and a sense of control to developing friendships.

Time

Two class periods.

Overview

Before we are able to develop meaningful friendships, we must know who we are, feel good about ourselves and feel in control of our lives.

In this lesson, students examine the concepts of self-identity *(I am)*, self-esteem *(I feel good about myself)* and internal locus or place of control *(I feel in control)* through group activities and journal entries.

Instructional Strategies	Journal writing, group discussion, worksheets, teacher-lecture.

Teacher Materials and Preparation

HAVE:

✓ Each student will need a loose-leaf notebook to keep a journal. (This should be separate from a note-taking notebook.)
✓ Overhead projector.
✓ Butcher paper, one piece for every three students.
✓ 8 1/2" x 22" piece of light-colored construction paper, one for each student.
✓ Magazines for collages.
✓ Scissors, one pair per student.
✓ Glue sticks or white glue, one for each student.

COPY:

✓ **Be Your Own Best Friend** worksheet, two for each student.
✓ **Looking at Your Life** journal entry, one for each student.
✓ **Looking at Your Life: A Closer Look** information sheet, one for each student.

MAKE:

✓ Transparency of **New Words**.
✓ Transparency of **Collage** *Example*.

REVIEW:

✓ **How to Use Journal Writing**.
✓ **Teacher Background Information**.

Procedure

■ Using the information in **How to Use Journal Writing**, explain the process to students. Tell them they will be keeping a journal while they are studying about friendships.

■ Explain to students that all of us need other people. We need to care and be cared for. We need to share ideas and experiences. In order to like and accept others, we must first like and accept ourselves.

This lesson deals with understanding and accepting ourselves.

Understanding who we are (self-identity), having positive feelings about ourselves (self-esteem) and feeling in control of our lives (internal locus of control) all provide foundations for our friendships with others.

Reveal the left-hand column of the **New Words** transparency, and discuss what students know about these terms. Use the **Teacher Background Information** on self-identity, self-esteem and locus of control to guide this discussion.

Divide the class into groups of three. Tell group members to discuss the meaning of the terms and come to a consensus about a definition for each term.

Give each group a piece of butcher paper and markers. Tell groups to record their definitions on the paper. Then ask each group to share its definitions with the class. Post the definitions in the classroom.

Then reveal the definitions on the right-hand side of the transparency and discuss as appropriate.

■ Distribute the **Be Your Own Best Friend** worksheet. Have students complete each of the sentences on the worksheet. Ask for volunteers to share personal responses on the worksheet as appropriate. Emphasize that when we know who we are, feel good about ourselves and feel in control of our lives, we are better able to establish friendships with others. Tell students to put the worksheet in their journals.

■ Distribute magazines to the class. Give each student a piece of construction paper, scissors and glue. Show students the **Collage Example** transparency. Tell students to write their names in large letters at the top of their papers. Then tell students to cut out pictures and words that describe themselves from magazines, and make a collage on the top half of the sheet. Post the collages on bulletin boards or tape them around the room for about a week.

Tell students that for the next week, they are invited to write nice comments on at least three students' papers as they come into the room each day. *Note*: Watch for sheets with only a few nice comments written on them. You or other teachers may discreetly write nice comments on these.

■ Distribute the **Looking at Your Life** journal entry. Tell students to answer the questions individually, or assign the journal entry as homework. When students have finished, ask for volunteers to share responses with the class.

Then distribute the student information sheet **Looking at Your Life: A Closer Look**. Use it as a guide for further discussion.

Evaluation

Have students complete another copy of the **Be Your Own Best Friend** worksheet. Have students write a short essay on either "How I Can Make Myself Happy" or "How I Can Keep From Being Bored."

HOW TO USE JOURNAL WRITING

What does a journal look like? How often should students write in their journals? What kinds of writing should they do on their own? How should they be graded?

A journal may be viewed as part diary and part class notebook. A diary is used to record the student's private thoughts and experiences, while a notebook is used to record the teacher's public thoughts and presentation of information. The journal is somewhere between a diary and a notebook.

Like a diary, the journal is written in the first person to record ideas, feelings and thoughts of importance to the writer. Like a notebook, the journal may focus on academic concerns the writer wishes to examine.

The journal encourages writers to become conscious, through written language, of what is happening to them—both personally and academically. The journal is also an indispensable tool in helping students expand their cognitive and verbal repertory (Kirby and Liner, 1981).

Journal writing is an effective strategy to give focus to an idea or to promote problem-solving skill building. Student responses in the journals can give teachers feedback on the degree of student comprehension.

Journals also have a special value in recording intellectual growth by preserving early, intermediate and final versions of individual thought on a particular issue. Each journal entry should be dated. This allows the writer to look back and recognize the process through which the finished thoughts emerged.

Students should use loose-leaf notebooks for their journals, so they can remove writings concerned with private thoughts and experiences before they hand in their notebooks.

When evaluating journals, points can be awarded for journal entries. However, journals should not be graded for composition errors. If points are not awarded, a minimum number of journal entries may be required for completion of module requirements. Teachers should collect journals two or three times during the module.

As you read each student's journal, personal comments may be written to the student. In this way, student journal writing provides an excellent technique for one-to-one teacher-student interaction.

In summary, journal writing is a useful teaching strategy that creates a climate for student exploration, discovery, problem solving and evaluation.

TEACHER BACKGROUND INFORMATION
Self-Identity, Self-Esteem and Locus of Control

Three important prerequisites to the development of meaningful friendships are self-identity, self-esteem and a sense of control.

The following expanded definitions should be helpful as you facilitate this lesson.

Self-identity is the way people describe themselves based on the roles they play and the personal attributes they think they possess. School achievement, perceived social status among peers and perceived self-worth within the family structure are some of the variables related to self-identity.

According to Erickson (1959), the predecessor of the development of identity in adolescence is the achievement of a sense of industry in middle childhood. If children succeed in tasks of the industry period, they will come to adolescence with confidence in their own worth and possess a set of skills that will foster the development of a positive identity (Marcia, 1980).

Adolescence is the crucial period, because for the first time the individual possesses the cognitive skills, the physical abilities and the social permission to construct a workable plan for an adult life and vocation (Garbarino, 1985).

According to Marcia (1980), achieving self-identity enables an individual to move ahead to the next stage of psychosocial development, that of forming stable, committed interpersonal relationships. Therefore, people must be friends with themselves before they can establish meaningful friendships with others.

Self-esteem is the level of satisfaction people feel with the roles they play and the personal attributes they think they possess. Self-esteem is a measure of how much people value themselves.

According to Erickson (1959), development of self-esteem is a lifelong process that begins in infancy and ends with death. During adolescence, individual self-perceptions may be more easily influenced by peers than by adults, since adolescents are keenly concerned with opinions of their peers (Beane, Lipka and Ludewig, 1980).

Locus (place) *of control* is a construct derived from Rotter's social learning theory (Wallston and Wallston, 1978) that is used to predict and explain specific behaviors. According to this theory, individuals are oriented to either an internal or an external control of behavior.

Internal (inside) *locus of control* refers to the belief that we can control what happens to us. A belief that one is controlled by luck, fate or powerful others is referred to as *external* (outside) *locus of control.* The generalized expectancies may have important consequences for how people respond to their social environment.

People with an internal locus of control are more self-directed. People with an external locus of control rely more on group support. However, current thinking indicates that locus of control may vary in individuals from situation to situation.

Sense of identity, positive self-esteem and internal locus of control are all important predictors of human behavior (Wallston and Wallston, 1978). As adolescents come to accept themselves and experience positive self-esteem, they will feel more in control of life situations.

New Words

Self-Identity: a sense of myself, separate from others, based on my past behaviors and what I expect to do in the future.

Self-Esteem: how much I value and care about myself.

Locus of Control: a way we explain specific human behaviors.

Internal Locus of Control: the belief that I am in control of what happens to me.

External Locus of Control: the belief that luck, fate or other people control my life.

Be Your Own Best Friend

Directions: In order to like and accept others, we must first like and accept ourselves. Write something about yourself for each of the numbered items by finishing the sentence.

1. **Self-Identity**

   I am:

2. **Self-Esteem**

   I feel good about myself:

3. **Internal Locus of Control**

   I have control over:

4. **External Locus of Control**

   I don't have control over (things that happen by chance or luck):

COLLAGE
Example

Name: _Susan Johnson_

Sporty
STYLE
Student

WHAT CAN TOP THE
COMFORT OF YOUR FAVORITE JEANS?

Friends...
Family
MUSIC MUSIC MUSIC MUSIC MUSIC MUSIC MUSIC

Nice Comments: a talented person

Funny   Good friend   Good in P.E.

        nice   Funny

Date _____

Looking at Your Life
Journal Entry

Directions: Please answer the following questions in your journal. Write your answers in complete sentences.

1. What do you like most about yourself?

2. What is the best thing that ever happened to you?

3. What did you do to make this happen?

4. Are you ever bored? If your answer is no, give three reasons you are not ever bored. If your answer is yes, describe three things you could do to keep from being bored.

5. Are you happy most of the time? If you are, give three reasons for being happy. If not, describe three things you could do to make yourself happy.

Looking at Your Life: A Closer Look

1. What do you like about yourself?

This is part of your self-esteem. Record some of the things you like about yourself. (Possible examples: your smile, your good disposition, the fact that you are a hard worker, your hair or eyes or your ability to do something well.)

2. What is the best thing that ever happened to you?

This question helps you learn more about your self-identity. (Possible examples: making an "A" in math class, becoming an Eagle Scout, painting a beautiful picture, getting invited to a special party, going camping, catching a big fish, building a great model, making the basketball team, being elected cheerleader.)

3. What did you do to make this happen?

Use some of the good things from Question 2 as you think about the following question. Did you set goals and work to make this happen? This question involves your *locus of control*. You might have been surprised when this good thing happened, but think back to see what you did to help it happen. The following are some examples:

- If you painted a beautiful picture, was it because you practiced painting many other pictures first?
- If you made the honor roll, was it because you studied hard?
- If you won a spelling contest, was it because you are always interested in spelling different words?
- If you were accepted into the choir, was it because you've practiced singing?
- If you won a free-throw shooting contest, was it because you practice free throws in your back yard?
- If you built a great model airplane, was it because you followed the directions and worked carefully?

4. Are you ever bored? If your answer is no, give three reasons you are not ever bored. If your answer is yes, describe three things you could do to keep from being bored.

If you are sometimes bored, could you use your *internal locus of control* to keep from being bored? For example, if you are bored waiting in line at the cafeteria, think of some ways you could keep from being bored. Here are some suggestions:

- Bring a book or magazine to read while waiting.
- Make plans for what you want to do this weekend.
- Think about a nice thing you can do for your parents or a friend today.
- Think about a compliment someone gave you yesterday or last week.
- Think about an essay you are going to write for English class.
- Imagine a drawing, painting or story you can create about yourself today.

Are you bored because you are waiting for something to happen to you? Do you need to be entertained by movies, television, tapes or other outside things? Can you entertain yourself?

People with *external locus of control* are those who wait for things to happen to them, as if by chance or luck. They are often bored. The challenge is to think of ways you can take control of your life and not be bored.

5. ***Are you happy most of the time? If you are, give three reasons for being happy. If not, describe three things you could do to make yourself happy.***

Maybe you are not especially happy at home because of problems there. If that is the case, why not choose to work hard on things you can have some control over at school? Even if some things make you unhappy, you can find other things to do to bring you happiness.

You can use your *internal locus of control* to help make up for things over which you have less control. Here are some examples:

- Study hard to earn good grades.
- Practice daily to make a sports team.
- Volunteer to work on the school newspaper.
- Practice to be in the choir or band.
- Work to become the basketball manager.
- Learn and practice to be a school photographer.
- Attend school council meetings and work to be elected representative.

Remember, people who are happy most of the time work to make themselves happy. People who *know who they are, like themselves* and *feel they have some control over their lives* find it easier to make and keep friends.

| LESSON 2 | # THE MEANING OF FRIENDSHIP |

Objectives

Students will be able to identify qualities they value in friends.

Time

Two class periods.

Overview

Trust, loyalty, warmth and the ability to keep confidences are qualities often valued in friends.

In this lesson, students use various activities, including journal writing and creating poetry, to increase their understanding of how they and others choose friends and develop friendships.

Instructional Strategies

Journal writing, group discussion, worksheets, interviewing, brainstorming, publishing in the classroom.

Teacher Materials and Preparation

HAVE:
- ✓ Overhead projector.

COPY:
- ✓ **Compliments** journal entry, one for each student.
- ✓ **The Inner Square** worksheet, one for each student.
- ✓ **Thoughts About the Inner Square** journal entry, one for each student.
- ✓ **My Close Friend** journal entry, one for each student.
- ✓ **Clustering** worksheet, one for each student.
- ✓ **Creating a Biopoem** worksheet, one for each student.
- ✓ **Looking at Friendship** worksheet, one for each student.

MAKE:
- ✓ Transparency of **The Inner Square** worksheet.
- ✓ Transparency of **Clustering** *Examples*.
- ✓ Transparency of **Biopoem** *Examples*.

Procedure

■ Distribute the **Compliments** journal entry. Have students think about feelings they had during the week when they read the nice comments on their collages. Explain to students that these were *compliments*. Compliments usually help us feel good about ourselves. Tell students to read the directions for the journal entry and answer the questions in their journals.

Ask for volunteers to share with the class one compliment that made them feel very special. Encourage students to give compliments freely and often to friends. Suggest that students review the compliments that were written on their collages when they are feeling down. Then have students place the **Compliments** journal entry in their journals.

■ Distribute **The Inner Square** worksheet. Project the worksheet transparency as you explain the activity to students. Point out the word ME in the center square. Tell students that this square represents them.

Tell students to write the names of their very close friends in the next square. Explain that parents or other family members could be included in this square, but for now encourage students to choose peers or friends close to their age.

Note: It may be hard for some students to cope with family members being named in the inner square in this activity. Students are at a development stage where they are exercising independence from parents. You may want to discuss this issue. Remind students that we all have different kinds of relationships with parents. For some, it is easy to discuss things with parents. For others, this is not true.

Tell students to write the names (or initials) of friends who are not very close friends in the third square. They should write the names of acquaintances in the fourth square. Explain that acquaintances are people they know, but don't consider friends.

When students have filled in the squares, distribute the **Thoughts About the Inner Square** journal entry. Tell students to read the directions and write the answers to the questions in their journals. Tell students to include the journal entry in their journals.

■ Distribute the **My Close Friend** journal entry. Tell students to choose one of the very close friends identified in the inner square and describe that person by answering the journal entry questions in their journals.

When students have completed their writing, divide the class into pairs and have students interview each other. Tell students to take turns asking each other the questions from the **My Close Friend** journal entry. Students can choose to share answers or to pass. But encourage pairs to find out if they have any similar answers. These answers can indicate similar qualities they like in friends.

■ Distribute the **Clustering** worksheet. Project a transparency of the **Clustering *Examples*** as you describe the activity to students. Ask each student to brainstorm words for the clustering worksheet.

Tell students to start with the name of a friend. Tell them to write the friend's name in the center of the page. Then tell students to brainstorm words that describe their friend and write these words in clusters on the worksheet.

■ Distribute the **Creating a Biopoem** worksheet and show the **Biopoem *Examples*** on an overhead transparency. Review the pattern and the sample poems with the class. Tell students to use words from their **Clustering** worksheets to fill in the biopoem pattern. This will create a biopoem about the friend named in the clustering activity.

When biopoems are finished, ask for volunteers to read their biopoems to the class. Publish the biopoems of students who are willing to share them with the class.

Evaluation

Distribute the **Looking at Friendship** worksheet. Ask students to complete it in class. Evaluate student worksheet responses to assess student understanding of the qualities they value in rewarding friendships.

Date _____

Compliments
Journal Entry

Directions: Please explain your feelings about the compliments you received by answering these questions in your journal. Write your answers in complete sentences.

1. Which compliments made you feel very special?

2. Why did each of these compliments make you feel special?

The Inner Square

Directions: Look at the word ME in the center square. In the inner square, write the names of your very close friends. In the next square, write the names of friends who are not very close friends. In the outside square, write the names of acquaintances—people you know but don't consider friends.

Date _____

Thoughts About the Inner Square
Journal Entry

Directions: Please answer the following questions in your journal. Write the answers in complete sentences.

1. How did you decide which friends were very close friends? (These were the friends in the square closest to you.)

2. How did you decide which friends were not close friends? (These were the friends in the third square.) Describe two differences in your feelings toward these friends and the acquaintances you named in the fourth square.

Date _____

My Close Friend
Journal Entry

Directions: Choose one close friend you identified on **The Inner Square** worksheet and describe him or her by answering the following questions in your journal. Write your answers in complete sentences.

1. List three of the things you most admire about this friend.

2. Do you feel close to this friend even if you don't see him or her every day? Explain why or why not.

3. Can you trust this friend? Give examples of times you've trusted her or him.

4. Has this friend ever let you down? Give examples of times this has happened.

5. Could you forgive this friend for letting you down or disappointing you? Explain.

Clustering

Examples

Directions: Write the name of a close friend in the center of the page. Then write down words that you think of when thinking about that person. Write all the words you think of—don't try to decide if they're good or bad. Write the words around the name. Circle each word when it is written. Draw lines and arrows to connect the words and the name.

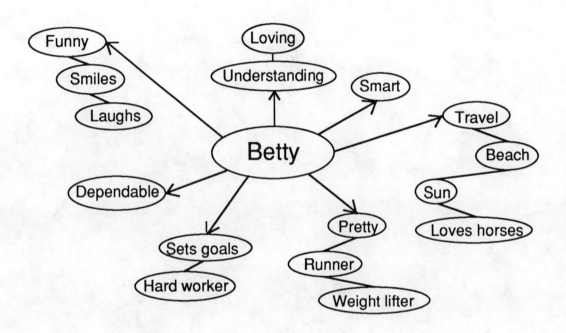

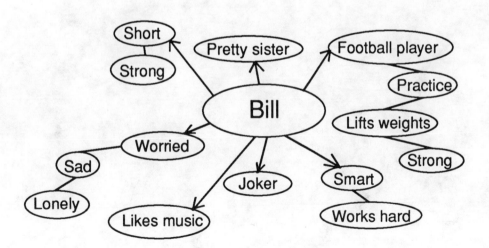

Clustering

Directions: Write the name of a close friend in the center of the page. Then write down words that you think of when thinking about that person. Write all the words you think of—don't try to decide if they're good or bad. Write the words around the name. Circle each word when it is written. Draw lines and arrows to connect the words and the name.

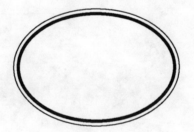

Biopoem
Examples

1. Betty

2. Pretty, dependable, smart, hard worker

3. Sister of Jane

4. Lover of horses, food, running

5. Who feels happy, responsible, loved

6. Who needs travel, fun, sunscreen

7. Who fears fences, sadness, dreary days

8. Who gives love, smiles, understanding

9. Who would like to see more caring, more smiles, more sun

10. Lives in the universe

11. Brown

Biopoem

Examples

1. Bill

2. Short, strong, smart, joker

3. Brother of a pretty sister

4. Lover of football, music, running

5. Who feels worried, sad, lonely

6. Who needs excitement, friends, fun

7. Who fears failure, frowns, life

8. Who gives money, compliments, time

9. Who would like to see the Super Bowl, Hawaii, world peace

10. Lives in a small town

11. Jones

Creating a Biopoem

Directions: Use the biopoem pattern and words from the **Clustering** worksheet to create a biopoem about a friend.

Biopoem Pattern
Line 1. (First name)
Line 2. (Four traits that describe character)
Line 3. (Relative—brother, sister, daughter, etc.) of _____
Line 4. Lover of _____(list three things or activities)
Line 5. Who feels _____(three items)
Line 6. Who needs _____(three items)
Line 7. Who fears _____(three items)
Line 8. Who gives _____(three items)
Line 9. Who would like to see _____(three items)
Line 10. Lives in _____
Line 11. (Last name)

Your Biopoem

1. _____

2. _____

3. _____

4. Lover of _____

5. Who feels _____

6. Who needs _____

7. Who fears _____

8. Who gives _____

9. Who would like to see _____

10. Lives in _____

11. _____

Looking at Friendship

1. Do you have more acquaintances, friends or very close friends?

   How many of each do you have? acquaintances _____ friends _____ very close friends _____

2. Is your very close friend loyal, warm, trustworthy? Can she or he keep a secret?

   _____yes _____no

   If no, why not?

3. If you don't see a very close friend for a long time, can you still be friends?

   _____yes _____no

4. Is this very close friend dependable?

   _____yes _____no

5. Do you spend time with this friend only because the two of you have common interests (such as playing sports or going to movies together)?

   _____yes _____no

6. Give two reasons you and your very close friend remain friends:

   1.
   2.

7. Is your biopoem a good description of your close friend?

   _____yes _____no

   If no, why not?

LESSON 3

THE FRIENDS YOU WANT

Objectives

Students will be able to describe ways that friends and peers influence personal choices and decisions.

Students will be able to identify some reasons to end a friendship.

Time

One class period.

Overview

While individual and group interactions provide valuable lessons in peer relationships, students should be aware that at this stage of their lives they may be especially vulnerable to external influence and peer pressures.

In this lesson, a worksheet focuses on personal and social issues facing students, and encourages them to examine their susceptibility to peer pressure. Another worksheet and roleplay activity allow students to practice skills to resist pressure.

| **Instructional Strategies** | Worksheets, roleplays, brainstorming, group discussion, journal writing. |

| **Teacher Materials and Preparation** | **COPY:**
✓ **The Influence of Friends** worksheet, one for each student.
✓ **Making Decisions About Peer Pressure** worksheet, one for each student.

PREPARE:
✓ **Roleplay Cards**, one for each group. |

Procedure

■ Distribute **The Influence of Friends** worksheet. Discuss the concept of peer pressure. Tell students that we all want to have friends. Sometimes this desire can lead us to do things we don't really want to do in order to please our friends. Explain that friends with whom we have little in common can sometimes try to pressure us to do things we do not really want to do.

Tell students to complete the worksheet and figure their scores. Explain that it is normal to start to have conflicts with parents about friends at their age. However, just because it is normal doesn't mean it is easy for parents or their children.

Remind students of the concepts discussed in Lesson 1 about being your own best friend. Point out that the same elements that help us create friendships—self-identity, self-esteem and feeling in control of our lives—can help us deal with and, if necessary, resist peer pressure.

■ Distribute the **Making Decisions About Peer Pressure** worksheet. Review the five decision-making steps. Tell students that developing and practicing these five steps can help them resist peer pressure. They can use these steps to refuse to do certain things with less risk of losing friendships they want to keep.

Review each of the five steps, emphasizing the following points:
1. *Identify the decision.* Know what decision you have to make. Then gather all the information you can get related to the

decision. Know the facts.
2. *Consider the choices.* Think of all the things you could do.
3. *Think about the consequences of each choice.* Make lists— in your head or wtitten down—of the good and bad things that could happen for each choice.
4. *Make the decision.* Choose the best action to take and then take action. It can be hard to act on a decision that isn't popular with your friends. Trust your decision. Suggest other activities you and your friends could do.
5. *Evaluate the decision.* Was it the right decision? Did it get the best results for you? If not, how can you change it? Would you make a different decision next time?

Tell students that when they refuse to behave in certain ways, they show others where they stand. Point out that they can suggest other activities and give their friends a choice. This places the burden of making a decision on the other person. Good friends will respect our feelings.

Emphasize that people who pressure us to do things that we know aren't right are really not good friends to us. Good friends help us feel better about ourselves. Have students roleplay the two scenarios on the worksheet and think about how the decision-making steps are used in the situations.

■ Divide the class into groups of four or five. Distribute the **Roleplay Cards.** Tell groups to use the five decision-making steps to create their own roleplays.

Then ask each group to present its roleplay to the class. After each presentation, lead the class in a discussion of each of the five steps used in the roleplay. If some of the steps have been omitted from the roleplay, have students brainstorm ways to include those steps.

Evaluation

Tell students to write in their journals what they learned about themselves while working on **The Influence of Friends** worksheet.

Tell students to write in their journals possible reasons to end a friendship. They should use full sentences for these and all journal entries. Review journals and assess students' ability to describe the ways peers influence them and their ability to identify reasons for ending a friendship.

The Influence of Friends

Directions: Respond to each question by circling *Yes* or *No*.

1. When you feel alone and lonely, do you have a hard time making decisions? (deciding whether to run for student council, try out for cheerleader, drill team or the basketball team; choosing your electives for next term) .... **Yes   No**

2. Have you ever felt pressured by friends to do something you really didn't want to do? (ride in a car with someone who is drinking or who doesn't have a driver's license; cheat on a test) .... **Yes   No**

3. Do you often decide to do certain things because you are afraid your friends will make fun of you or not like you? (playing football instead of chess; going to a party instead of visiting your grandfather) .... **Yes   No**

4. Do you sometimes act a certain way because you are afraid your friends will not like you or will make fun of you? (laugh at a dirty joke even though you don't think it's funny; smoke cigarettes even though you don't like them) .... **Yes   No**

5. Do you have some of the same goals in life as most of your friends? (getting a good job; doing well in school; not using drugs; planning to graduate from high school) .... **Yes   No**

6. Have you reached fewer of your personal goals since you have started going places with your current friends? (not doing well in school, not staying away from tobacco) .... **Yes   No**

7. Are you spending most of your free time with the same small group of friends? .... **Yes   No**

8. Is it hard for you to make new friends outside of your current group of friends? .... **Yes   No**

9. Do your parents disapprove of your current group of friends? .... **Yes   No**

10. Would you feel guilty if you stopped being a friend to some friends who don't share your values? (friends who goof off at school or lie to their parents) .... **Yes   No**

Scoring: The more *yes* responses you have, the more likely you are to be influenced by your friends.

8-10   Very likely. Your friends are having a great deal of influence upon your life.
4-7   Somewhat likely. Your friends are sometimes influencing the decisions you are making.
1-3   Not very likely. You are in control of your life.

Making Decisions About Peer Pressure

Five Decision-Making Steps

1. Identify the decision.
2. Consider the choices.
3. Think about the consequences of each choice.
4. Make the decision.
5. Evaluate the decision.

Bill and Tim meet in the hallway between classes.

Bill: Let's hang out at the Quick Mart after school.

Tim: What are we going to the Quick Mart for?

Bill: I hear a big bag of M&Ms calling me. You could talk to the clerk while I grab it.

Tim: That's stealing. We could get into a lot of trouble if we do that. Why don't we go over to my house after school? I made some chocolate chip cookies last night. We can pig out on those.

Bill: Hey, man, don't you want to go with me?

Tim: I don't want to get into trouble for a bag of candy. I'll wait for you until 3:30 by the gym. I hope you'll decide to come over to my house. See you later.

Janet calls Kendra at home to talk about going to a basketball game in the new gym tomorrow night.

Janet: I have an idea. When we go the the basketball game tomorrow night, let's be the first to write on the walls in the new restroom.

Kendra: You must be really bored, girl. You know how much trouble we could get in for doing that.

Janet: Oh, come on, it'll be fun to make the first marks on that fresh paint.

Kendra: I want to see the basketball game, and I don't want to get in trouble. If we got caught, we wouldn't stand a chance of getting on the yearbook staff. Ms. Taylor's choosing the new staff members next month. I hope we both make it. It would be fun to work together on the yearbook next year. Let's not take a chance on getting into trouble. Think about it. I'll see you tomorrow at school.

The decision-making steps were adapted from *Into Adolescence: Avoiding Drugs* (ETR Associates, 1990.)

ROLEPLAY CARDS

Directions: Cut apart on dotted lines. Paste on cards for students to use in class (optional).

Characters: _____

_____

_____

Situation _____

_____

_____

5 Steps _____

_____

_____

_____

_____

Characters: _____

_____

_____

Situation _____

_____

_____

5 Steps _____

_____

_____

_____

_____

LESSON 4

DEVELOPING CLOSE FRIENDSHIPS

Objectives

Students will be able to describe important skills to use in developing close friendships.

Time

Two class periods.

Overview

Close friendships do not happen by accident. They are created and nurtured.

In this lesson, students study four important friendship skills. Roleplays illustrate negative and positive uses of each of the four skills. Students then work in dyads to create their own roleplay situations for presentation to the class. Brainstorming is used to identify the friendship skills demonstrated in the roleplays.

Instructional Strategies	Teacher lecture, group discussion, roleplays, brainstorming, journal writing.

Teacher Materials and Preparation	**HAVE:** ✓ Overhead projector. ✓ Video equipment for taping and screening roleplays (optional). **COPY:** ✓ **Confidences Build Trust** *Roleplay*, one for each student. ✓ **Understanding and Empathy** *Roleplay*, one for each student. ✓ **Active Listening** *Roleplay*, one for each student. ✓ **"I" Statements** *Roleplay*, one for each student. **MAKE:** ✓ Transparency of **Four Friendship Skills**. **PREPARE:** ✓ Write the four friendship skills on slips of paper for random student drawing from a hat or box. Make enough slips to distribute one slip to every two students.

Procedure	■ Conduct a short lecture-discussion about the importance of close friendships, using **Teacher Background Information** as a guide. Tell students that there are four important skills that help us develop close friendships. Use the **Four Friendship Skills** transparency and **Teacher Background Information** to continue a discussion about each of these skills. ■ Distribute the four roleplay situations: **Confidences Build Trust, Understanding and Empathy, Active Listening**, and **"I" Statements**. Explain that each roleplay demonstrates the use of a friendship skill. Ask for volunteers to roleplay the scenarios. Discuss each roleplay. Ask students to identify places in the roleplay where a specific friendship skill was used.

■ Divide class into dyads. Have each dyad draw one friendship skill from the hat or box. Tell each dyad to create a roleplay that illustrates positive and negative ways to use this skill.

Following presentation of the roleplays, brainstorm with the class to identify appropriate and inappropriate use of the four friendship skills.

Optional: Allow students to practice the roleplays and videotape them.

Evaluation

Have students write in their journals their own description of the skills needed to develop a close friendship. Tell them to give examples of the skills. They should use full sentences. Review journals for descriptions of each of the four friendship skills.

TEACHER BACKGROUND INFORMATION
Friendship Skills

Close friendships are important at all stages of life. However, friendships are especially important during adolescence. Friendships ease the transition from childhood to adulthood. According to Erickson (1959), affiliation with peers provides many of the essential experiences and opportunities for self-definition required for the formation of self-identity. (See **Teacher Background Information** in Lesson 1 for additional information on self-identity.)

In today's society, friends often fill a void created by a troubled family situation. Friends share their feelings to help each other resolve personal and interpersonal conflicts and problems (Garbarino, 1985).

Page (1989) found that adolescents who have problems developing and maintaining friendships are more susceptible to peer pressure and are more likely to participate in high-risk behaviors (e.g., smoking and dipping, using alcohol and other drugs). Adolescent girls frequently enter into sexual relationships when they are searching for close (intimate) friendships.

The development of a close friendship requires the following essential skills: the ability to keep confidences, which develops trust; the ability to understand and empathize with others; the ability to practice active listening; and the ability to communicate by using "I" statements.

Webster defines *confidence* as "full trust; belief in trustworthiness or reliability of a person or thing." Webster defines *trust* as (1) "the state of being relied upon, or the state of one to whom something is entrusted"; or (2) "relying upon the honesty, integrity and justice of another person."

The ability to keep confidences and the ability to trust another person are vital to the development of close friendships. Close friendships can evolve only when each person in the friendship experiences mutual feelings of loyalty and trust. When trust is violated, the friendship is often severely damaged.

Webster defines *understanding* as "a mutual comprehension." To understand can mean "to know thoroughly" or "to have a sympathetic rapport with." *Empathy* is defined as "the ability to share in another's emotions, thoughts or feelings."

Understanding and empathy involve what some have called "role-taking" (Weinstein, 1969). In order to empathize, one must "take the role of another" or "walk in another's shoes" and be able to accurately predict another person's thoughts and feelings. The ability to understand and empathize enables an adolescent to gain social competence through meaningful interpersonal relationships.

Active listening is a difficult skill to acquire. However, it is a vital skill because it helps develop understanding and empathy. Active listening also helps the person being listened to feel worthy of another's time and undivided attention.

Active listening means to concentrate upon listening to what another person is saying. Active listening skills include the following four steps:

- establishing eye contact,
- listening without interruption,
- listening without thinking about the response that will be made, and
- learning to empathize with others.

Learning to use "I" instead of "you" statements is essential when confronting problems or concerns that occur in a friendship. Using "I" statements allows us to voice our concerns in a nonthreatening manner. This increases chances of resolution of the problem addressed.

"You" statements frequently cause others to feel they are being blamed. They then become defensive. When you are being defensive, it is very difficult to do active listening.

"I" statements effectively communicate concerns and feelings, help us empathize with another's feelings and create an atmosphere more conducive to resolving misunderstandings. Being able to disagree and resolve problems is important in the development and maintenance of a close friendship.

Four Friendship Skills

1. Keep Secrets and Build Trust

2. Develop Understanding and Empathy

3. Practice Active Listening Skills

★ Establish eye contact with the other person.

★ Listen to the person without interruption.

★ Listen to the person without thinking of what you will say next.

★ Empathize with the person as he or she is speaking.

4. Use "I" Statements

Confidences Build Trust
Roleplay

One night at the band concert, Janelle told Debbie, her best friend, that she liked Jason a lot. This was a secret. Janelle didn't want anyone else to know.

The next morning, Debbie and Betty had the following conversation while walking to class.

Betty: I saw you and Janelle telling secrets at the band concert last night. What did Janelle tell you? Come on, you can tell me. I can keep a secret.

Debbie: Betty, I can't tell you. Janelle wants me to keep what she told me a secret. I promised not to tell anyone.

Betty: Come on. Tell me—please. I won't tell anyone. I promise.

Debbie: Okay, if you promise not to tell anyone else. Did you know Janelle really likes Jason? She told me she did. But she doesn't want Jason to know. Please don't tell anyone else. She'll hate me if she finds out I told you!

Betty later told another friend. Then Jason heard the secret. Do you think Janelle felt betrayed? What should Debbie have done when Betty asked her to tell Janelle's secret?

Roleplay the situation again. This time, Debbie should refuse to tell Betty the secret.

Debbie: I can't tell Janelle's secret. She asked me not to tell anyone. You wouldn't want me to tell one of your secrets, would you? I'm sorry, but I can't tell you anything about what we talked about.

Understanding and Empathy
Roleplay

Paul is your good friend. Paul's dad is a fire fighter. A rumor is going around school that Paul's dad has been injured while fighting a fire. Paul is very upset. He can't reach his mother by phone. He can't leave school until he can find a family member to come pick him up. As a close friend, how would you empathize with Paul?

Examples:

➔ Be an active listener as Paul tells you how worried he is.

➔ Put yourself in Paul's situation. How would you feel if you were Paul and this was happening to you?

➔ Ask the teacher if you can go with Paul to the principal's office to try again to call his mother.

➔ Try to reassure Paul. Explain that rumors are often worse than actual happenings, but you can understand his worry and concern.

Active Listening
Roleplay

Robert is 12 years old. His mother and father have been divorced for a long time. Last year Robert's mom married a man named Nick. Robert has lived with his mom (and now with Nick) in the same house ever since he was a baby. Robert sees his dad one weekend a month and spends one month in summer and part of Christmas vacation with him.

Last week, Robert's mom and Nick told him they were moving into a new house, leaving his neighborhood and school. Robert is telling a close friend about his feelings.

Robert: I am very worried about moving into a new neighborhood and going to a new school. I like the new house, but I am sad about leaving you and my other friends at school. I like being on the basketball team here and being on the honor roll. I'm afraid I won't get on the basketball team there. And what if the teachers aren't nice in the new school, and I don't make the honor roll? What if I don't meet any new friends? Even if I do, I know I won't have a good friend like you.

As Robert's close friend, how would you help him feel less afraid and alone?

Examples:

→ Listen to Robert's worries. Establish eye contact and listen to what he is saying without interrupting or thinking about what you will say to him.

→ Tell him you understand how he feels and that you are also sad he is going to a new school.

→ Reassure him about the new school. (If he is a good student, he will make the honor roll.)

→ Tell him you will still be his friend. (You can call each other and sometimes do things together on weekends.)

"I" Statements
Roleplay

Fran and Jennie are best friends. However, Fran ignored Jennie all day. After school, Jennie phoned Fran to ask what's wrong. The following conversation took place.

Jennie: Fran, what's wrong? You didn't talk to me at school today. In fact, you seemed to ignore me.

Fran: I'm mad. You're my best friend. But you took Beth to eat pizza and then you went to a movie, and you didn't ask me. You told me you were my best friend. *You* can't be trusted. I'm mad because *you* treated me like that.

Jennie: Going out for pizza and a movie with Beth and her mom was my mom's idea, not mine. And besides, that doesn't mean I'm not your friend.

Fran: It's your fault. Why didn't you tell your mom you wanted me to go too?

Jennie: Fran, I'm sorry you're hurt. I couldn't tell my mom that. My mom and Beth's mom work together, so Mom wanted the four of us to get together.

Fran: *You* just don't care anymore. *You* hurt my feelings.

Even though Fran's feelings are hurt, how could she have used "I" instead of "you" statements to communicate her feelings to Jennie?

Roleplay the situation again. This time, Fran should use "I" statements to communicate her feelings.

Fran: I stayed away from you at school today because my feelings are hurt. I found out you took Beth out for pizza and a movie and didn't ask me. *I* thought we were best friends. *I* can't understand why this happened.

Jennie: I didn't mean to hurt your feelings. My mom and I did go out with Beth and her mom for pizza and a movie. But it was my mom's idea to do this, not mine. My mom and Beth's mom work together, and they arranged the whole thing. You're still my best friend. I would never hurt your feelings on purpose.

Fran: Oh, I didn't know it was your mom's idea. I misunderstood the whole thing. I'm sorry I didn't talk to you at school today. Let's meet before school tomorrow and walk to math class together.

<table>
<tr>
<td>

LESSON

5

</td>
<td>

FRIENDSHIP THROUGH THE YEARS

</td>
</tr>
</table>

Objectives

Students will be able to describe the importance of friendship at different stages of life.

Time

Three class periods.

Overview

Adolescents can learn a lot about the meaning of friendship from parents, other adults and senior citizens.

In this lesson, students interview parents or other adults at home about friendship. During one class period, students prepare for a classroom visit from a group of senior citizens. Students interview the seniors in small groups to discuss the lifelong significance of friendship. As a follow-up, students write thank-you letters to the seniors who visited.

Instructional Strategies

Teacher lecture, group discussion, interviewing, worksheets, journal writing.

Teacher Materials and Preparation

HAVE:
- ✓ Overhead projector (optional).
- ✓ Butcher paper or blank transparencies to record student answers.
- ✓ Pen for marking on transparency or butcher paper.

COPY:
- ✓ **Interview with Senior Friends** worksheet, several for each student.
- ✓ **Interview with Parent** worksheet, one for each student.
- ✓ **Parent Interview Summary** journal entry, one for each student.
- ✓ **Senior Interview Summary** journal entry, one for each student.

MAKE:
- ✓ Transparency of **Interview with Senior Friends** (optional).

PREPARE:
- ✓ Invite five senior citizens to visit the classroom to be interviewed by the students. Choose seniors whose ages range from middle 50s to 70s or 80s. Invite individuals you know, or arrange for five members of a retirement group to visit the class. It is important to have a variety of ages represented.

REVIEW:
- ✓ **Teacher Background Information**.

Procedure

■ On the day prior to the seniors' visit, prepare the students for this visit by discussing some characteristics of seniors in our society. (See **Teacher Background Information**.) Use some of the following questions to guide this discussion:
- How many people in the United States lived to be 100 years or older in 1985?

- How many people do you think will live to be 100 years or older by the year 2000?
- Do you think most seniors are sick a lot?
- Do you think most seniors are lonely?
- Do you think most seniors are grumpy?
- Do you think seniors like to work?
- Do you think seniors care about other people?

■ Distribute the **Interview with Senior Friends** worksheet. Ask students to brainstorm answers the senior friends might give during their interviews. Record these predicted answers on butcher paper or on a transparency of the worksheet. Allow students to share stories about their great-grandparents or other senior friends. Tell students to save the worksheets for the next day's interviews.

■ Introduce the senior friends who are visiting the class. Divide the class into groups of five. Place one senior in the center of each group of students. Students should be sitting at their desks with the desks grouped in a circle.

Tell students to take out the **Interview with Senior Friends** worksheet. Distribute extra worksheets so each student has one worksheet for each senior visiting the class. Allow each student in the group to ask the senior one question from the worksheet.

When each group has asked all five questions, ask the seniors to move to another circle until they have visited with all the groups. When the exercise is done, thank the seniors for their visit.

■ Distribute the **Interview with Parent** worksheet. Ask each student to conduct this interview as homework. Tell students they can interview either a parent or another adult with whom they have a close relationship.

■ When students have completed both the senior interviews and the parent interviews, discuss the interviews in class. Ask students to answer the following questions during the class discussion. Record the answers on transparencies or on butcher paper.
- Describe one new thing you learned about friendship when interviewing your parent.
- Describe one new thing you learned about friendship when interviewing the seniors.
- Compare the friendship characteristics your parent and the

seniors said they most admired with the friendship characteristics you identified in Lesson 2, *The Meaning Of Friendship.*

- Compare and contrast the reasons friends are important to your parent and to seniors with the reasons friends are important to you.
- Identify examples of peer pressure related by your parent. Did you know adults experienced peer pressure?
- Identify examples of peer pressure related by the seniors. Did you know seniors experienced peer pressure?

Evaluation

Distribute the **Parent Interview Summary** and **Senior Interview Summary** journal entries. Tell students to write summaries of their interviews. Evaluate student responses for understanding of the lifelong importance of friendships. Tell students to include these entries in their journals.

Follow-up/ Extension

Have students write thank-you letters to the seniors who visited the class.

TEACHER BACKGROUND INFORMATION
Learning from Seniors

The population of America is living longer (growing older). According to the U.S. Bureau of the Census, more than 25,000 people lived to be 100 years or older in 1985. By the year 2000, an estimated 100,000 people in the United States will live to be 100 years or older.

Not only are people living longer, the majority of seniors are generally healthy. Many older citizens continue to exercise regularly. They are usually wise consumers of food and have more positive health habits than their younger counterparts. Seniors are less likely to drink or smoke.

Older people are freed from pressure to prove themselves. They have time to pursue interests and hobbies they had no time for earlier in life. Many seniors reach out to others as they often get involved in political and social causes. Some seniors still work for pay to supplement their income. Others work as volunteers.

Since seniors have lived longer, they are generally wiser. They may worry less about what other people think of them. They are often psychologically better off than younger people. They worry less about themselves and how they look than young people. They generally have higher self-esteem and are not as lonely as is sometimes reported.

Seniors make great friends. Adolescents and seniors can learn a lot from each other. Despite their age differences, adolescents and seniors can enjoy meaningful friendships.

Interview with Senior Friends

_____

Senior Friend's Name

1. Name the activity that you most enjoy doing with a friend (going to a movie, going to church, taking a walk, playing cards).

2. Do you have a friend that you have had for ten years or more?

   If so, why do you think you have remained friends so long?

3. Name your best female and best male friend.

   Name the friendship quality that you most admire in each of these friends.

4. Compared to when you were a teenager, are your friends:

   → more important today?

   → less important today?

   → just as important today?

5. Do your friends influence your decisions about the clothes you wear and the places you go?

   Give examples.

Interview with Parent

_____

Name of person interviewed

1. Name the activity that you most enjoy doing with a friend (going to a movie, going to church, taking a walk, playing cards).

2. Do you have a friend that you have had for ten years or more?

   If so, why do you think you have remained friends so long?

3. Name your best female and best male friend.

   Name the friendship quality that you most admire in each of these friends.

4. Compared to when you were a teenager, are your friends:
   → more important today?
   → less important today?
   → just as important today?

5. Do your friends influence your decisions about the clothes you wear and the places you go?

   Give examples.

Date _____

Parent Interview Summary
Journal Entry

Directions: Please write a summary of your interview with your parent (or other close adult). Write your answers in complete sentences. Be sure to answer these questions:

1. Describe one or two reasons your parent gave for having long-term friendships (of ten years or longer).

2. Describe two ways your parent said friends influence what he or she wears and where he or she goes (peer pressure).

3. In what ways are your parent's friendships and your friendships alike?

4. How are they different?

Date _____

Senior Interview Summary
Journal Entry

Directions: Please write a summary of your interviews with seniors. Write your answers in complete sentences. Be sure to answer these questions:

1. Describe one or two reasons the seniors identified as reasons for having long-term friendships (of ten years or longer).

2. Describe two ways the seniors said their friends influence the way they dress or where they go (peer pressure).

3. In what ways are the seniors' friendships and your friendships alike?

4. How are they different?

5. Which of your predictions of the seniors' answers were correct?

6. What surprised you most about the seniors' friendships?

LESSON 6

WHAT I LEARNED ABOUT FRIENDSHIP

Objectives

Students will be able to analyze the importance of friendship to them.

Time

One class period.

Overview

In this lesson, students play a game as a review and culminating activity. As a homework assignment, students analyze in their journals what they learned about friendship.

Instructional Strategies

Games, journal writing.

Teacher Materials and Preparation

COPY:
✓ **What I Learned** journal entry, one for each student.

REVIEW:
✓ The Friendship Game *Rules*.
✓ The Friendship Game *Puzzles*.

Procedure

■ Begin the class by playing *The Friendship Game*. Explain the rules of the game and divide the class into two teams. The teams should be evenly balanced, with comparable knowledge and skills. Students may either sit at their desks or stand in rows on both sides of the room. Have one student from each team draw a number to see which team begins. Play the game for at least 20 minutes.

■ When students begin to tire of the game, distribute the **What I Learned** journal entry. Tell students to describe in their journals what they've learned about friendship.

Evaluation

Review the **What I Learned** journal entry for students' understanding and insight about the importance of friendship.

THE FRIENDSHIP GAME
Rules

Draw lines on the chalkboard to represent the letters of a word or phrase (the puzzle). Draw a box on each side of the chalkboard to record each team's points. Teams score one point for each letter of the puzzle that is guessed correctly. Draw a box on the chalkboard below the puzzle to hold the used letters.

One student at a time guesses a letter of the puzzle. If the first student correctly guesses a letter, his or her team scores a point. The next student on the same team then guesses a letter. As long as team members guess letters correctly, that team keeps the turn. One team may continue without losing a turn until a puzzle is solved.

When a student guesses a letter that is not in the word, the letter is placed on the *used letter board*. The other team then gets a turn.

Students have only three seconds to guess a letter. They may buy vowels that cost one point each. Points used to buy vowels are erased from the points the team has earned.

Only the team that successfully solves the puzzle receives the points earned. Use a tiebreaker if teams are tied when time for the game is over.

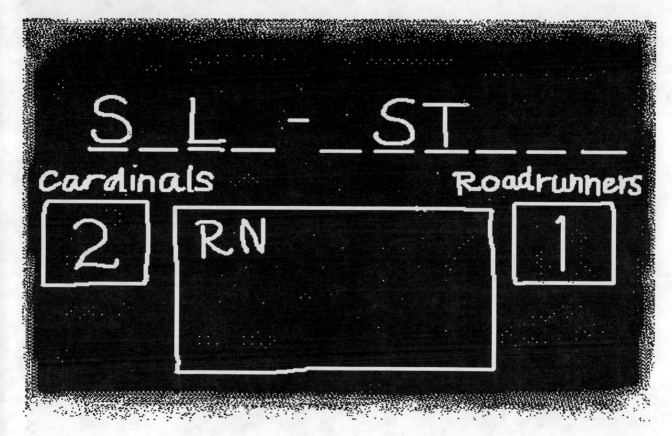

THE FRIENDSHIP GAME
Puzzles

Example:
SELF ESTEEM

USE "I" INSTEAD OF "YOU" STATEMENTS

SELF-IDENTITY

SELF-ESTEEM

LOCUS OF CONTROL

INTERNAL LOCUS OF CONTROL

EXTERNAL LOCUS OF CONTROL

FOUR FRIENDSHIP SKILLS

CONFIDENCES BUILD TRUST

UNDERSTANDING AND EMPATHY

ACTIVE LISTENING SKILLS

BIOPOEM

CLUSTERING

THE INNER SQUARE

GIVING COMPLIMENTS

MY CLOSE FRIEND

JOURNAL WRITING

SENIOR FRIENDS

BE YOUR OWN BEST FRIEND

HANDLING PEER PRESSURE

THE INFLUENCE OF FRIENDS

STATE THE CONSEQUENCES

NAME THE TROUBLE

ASK QUESTIONS. CHECK IT OUT.

SUGGEST ALTERNATIVES

LEAVE AND LEAVE THE DOOR OPEN

Date _____

What I Learned
Journal Entry

Directions: Think about ten things that you learned are important to you about friendship. Explain each of these things in your journal. Write your answers in complete sentences. You may write several sentences for each of the ten things.

GLOSSARY

acceptance
The act of agreeing or giving approval.

active listening
Listening to others without interrupting or allowing your thoughts to wander. Giving another your undivided attention.

confidence
Trusting or believing in or relying on the honesty and integrity of a person.

empathy
The act of putting yourself in another's place in order to share the other's thoughts or feelings.

enjoy
To get joy or pleasure from.

external locus (place) of control
The belief that you are controlled by luck or fate or other people.

internal locus (place) of control
The belief that you can shape and control your own destiny.

locus (place) of control
A way of explaining specific human behaviors.

peer pressure
The influence you feel from others your age that persuades you to do something or act in a certain way.

respect
To hold in high regard.

roleplay
To act out an open-ended scene; a way to learn about communicating ideas.

self-esteem
A measure of how much you value yourself.

self-identity
The way you describe yourself, based on the roles you play and the traits you think you possess.

sharing
Having or using in common with others.

support
To provide for, emotionally or physically; to take sides with, during discussion.

trust
To place confidence in another person.

understanding
The act of knowing and empathizing with another person.

REFERENCES

Beane, J., Lipka, R. and Ludewig, J. 1980. Synthesis of research on self-concept. *Educational Leadership* 38:109.

Erickson, E. 1959. Identity and the life cycle. *Psychological Issues* 1:171.

Fulwiler, R., ed. 1985. Journals across the disciplines. *To compose: Teaching writing in the high school.* Chelmsford, Mass.: Northeast Regional Exchange, Inc.

Fulwiler, T. 1987. *Teaching with writing.* Portsmouth, NH: Boynton/ Cook.

Garbarino, J. 1985. *Adolescent development: An ecological perspective.* Columbus, Ohio: Charles Merrill.

Gere, A., ed. 1985. *Roots in the sawdust: Writing to learn across the disciplines.* Urbana, Ill.: National Council of Teachers of English.

Howard, J. 1978. *Families.* New York: Simon and Schuster.

Kirby, D. and Liner, T. 1981. *Inside out: Developmental strategies for teaching writing*. Portsmouth, N.H.: Boynton/Cook.

Marcia, J. 1980. Identity in adolescence. In *Handbook of adolescent psychology*, ed. by J. Adelson. New York: John Wiley & Sons.

Mayer, H., Lester, N. and Pradl, G. 1983. *Learning to write, writing to learn*. Portsmouth, N.H.: Boynton/Cook.

Nelms, B. 1987. Response and responsibility: Reading, writing, and social studies. *Elementary School Journal* 5:586.

Page, R. 1989. Shyness as a risk factor for adolescent substance abuse. *Journal of School Health* 59: 432-435.

Wallston, B. and Wallston, K. 1978. Locus of control and health: A review of the literature. *Health Education Monographs* 6:107-114.

Weinstein, E. 1969. The development of interpersonal competence. In *Handbook of socialization theory and research*, ed. by D. Goslow. Chicago: Rand McNally.

About the Author

Emogene Fox, EdD, is an associate professor of health education at the University of Central Arkansas in Conway. She holds a BSE in English and an MSE in health education. She has taught English and health education in grades 7 through 12. She has also written a variety of health education curriculum materials for the University of Arkansas Cooperative Extension Service, including 4-H program materials. In addition to university teaching responsibilities, Dr. Fox coordinates student internships and contributes articles and reviews to professional publications.

Reviewers of
Into Adolescence: Making and Keeping Friends

Debbie Baker
Health Education Teacher
Bald Knob Public Schools
Bald Knob, AR

Lisa Ann DiPlacido, MS
Drug/Alcohol Prevention Specialist
Greater Erie Community Action Committee
Erie, PA

Gregory D. Gordon
Lead Teacher
American Indian Education and Cultural
Organization
Martinez, CA

Louise Mann, MEd, MAR
Director of Human Growth and Development
Renbrook School
West Hartford, CT

Eloise L. Miller, MEd
Health Education Consultant
Anoka-Hennepin District #11
Anoka, MN

John Pence, PhD
Principal
Newport Middle School
Newport, OR

Julie Taylor
Associate Training Director
ETR Associates
Santa Cruz, CA

Nancy Winkler, MSE
Human Growth and Development
Coordinator
CESA #6
Oshkosh, WI